YOU STARTED

your

BLOG

NOW WHAT…?

~~~

6 Steps to Blogging Bliss…

by Gundi Gabrielle

First Edition Paperback: February 2017

ISBN-13: 978-1542965903
ISBN-10: 154296590X

The Cataloging-In-Publication Data is on file with the Library of Congress.

*This is a **SassyZenGirl** Guide*

FREE Bonus

Hi there!

Great to meet you! - I am excited to help you grow your first blog!

As a *thank you* for purchasing my book, I prepared a FREE report that's exclusive to you, my readers.

How to pick a marketable Domain Name that will rank well and create a real buzz in the blogosphere

Just go to:

SassyZenGirl.com/Domain-Name

Picking a marketable Domain Name will be one of the most important decisions you will ever make. Sure, you can always change it later, but why not pick an awesome name right from the start?

In this FREE Report I compiled the advice from the top dogs in the blogging & marketing business to help you get started the right way and save you years of frustration.

Enjoy!

Gundi Gabrielle

TABLE OF CONTENTS

You started Your Blog - Now What.....?

This is probably the #1 question every new blogger asks once the technical set up is completed.

It's exciting to become a blogger and share with the world - but how exactly do you do that?

How do you get people to read your stuff? - How do you spread the word and get regular subscribers?

Many bloggers also struggle to decide what to blog about. What is a good topic and how do you research that?

And......is there - maybe - a way to make money with your new blog?

These and many other questions will be answered in this book with step-by-step instructions on where to go from here.

If you haven't started your blog yet, CLICK HERE to learn the technical steps for setting up a blog:

SassyZenGirl.com/Blogging-Guide

It is the first book in this blogging series and has helped thousands of people to get started. It can do the same for you.

For more in-depth training specifically on traffic generation, there are 3 more volumes on:

* SEO/How to rank in Google
* Social Media Marketing
* Kindle Publishing

For now, lets start with the basics, what to focus on right now - and what *not*!

What NOT to focus on in the Beginning:

A lot of new bloggers get lost in details, things that aren't really that important and then get frustrated when no one reads their awesome content.

Why?

Because they didn't focus on the #1 priority for any blog: Sharing with an Audience!

Instead they spent most of their time - often weeks - on:

1) Trying out different themes

2) Spending money on expensive, complicated themes and spending days and weeks trying to figure out how to use them

3) Spending a lot of time on blog design - making it look "pretty" or "perfect"

Yes, it is important to have a nice looking blog. It is your baby and you want to impress people. Understandable!

But - unless you do the initial work and learn how to:

* Research what people are actually interested in

* Define who your audience is

* How to find post topics that can go viral

and most importantly

* The writing style of blogging

all your other efforts will most likely be in vain.

Also, as you get your bearings as a blogger, your niche, design, and the overall feel of your blog will probably change or at least evolve over time.

It's a work in progress, a journey - and that's part of the fun.

First things first:

Please release yourself from the notion that your blog has to look "perfect" first, before you can focus on attracting an audience and learn how to write.

All you need in the beginning is a design that's clean and functional. Then focus on the other parts in this book and once that is working, you can go back to fine tuning your blog design.

By then, you will be much more experienced with *Wordpress* and have a better understanding of what features you may need that are unique to your niche and style.

It is very easy to change themes along the way. Just stay in the regular *Wordpress* editor when you write posts, and a new theme will simply take over.

Start with something simple. A theme you can easily learn in a day, one that doesn't have too many features with complicated names you don't understand.

Free themes are perfectly sufficient in the beginning and if you like the theme, you can always upgrade to the pro version with more extensive features and tech support. In most cases, an upgrade doesn't cost more than $10-15. But once again, you don't need that right away.

Instead, follow these 3 steps to get started:

1) Pick one of the free Wordpress.org themes

2) Go to *Youtube* and search for a tutorial for that theme.

3) Watch the tutorial and start setting up a few pages as well as the basic design of your blog: colors, fonts, styles etc.

For starters, you need a *Blog* page, an *About* page and a *Contact* page. If you sell products or offer services, then obviously add pages for those as well.

You can easily set this up in an hour - 2 tops. That's why video tutorials are so awesome. There is no faster way to learn, and you don't waste time trying around and getting frustrated.

Once again, don't worry about being perfect or making mistakes. You will definitely make mistakes and that's ok. Everybody does - even the top bloggers in the business - and it's usually not a big deal.

Just get started, write your first post, even just a short greeting to the world - and hit "Publish".

This will be a big milestone - the moment when you officially become a blogger.

Take time to celebrate!

Then start reading this book - shouldn't take more than an hour - and apply the steps described here:

CHAPTER 1 - Finding a Blog Topic that People Actually Want to Read...

CHAPTER 2 - How to Find Viral Blog Post Ideas

CHAPTER 3 - The Writing Style of Blogging

CHAPTER 4 - How to Drive Traffic to your Blog

CHAPTER 5 - How to convert traffic into Subscribers

CHAPTER 6 - How to Make Money with Your Blog

That's it.

Not complicated, and yet, understanding those basic principles will put you WAY ahead of 95% of new bloggers.

You won't be running a "Ghost Town" - that's what we call blogs with no visitors, no audience. And sadly, that's the vast majority.

Don't be one of them.

The strategies I am sharing here, are not my own "inventions". I learned them from the best of the best, applied them consistently, and built successful blogs within just a few months.

These strategies work, there is no need to reinvent the wheel.

It is much easier to follow others who were successful - people like the guys from *SmartBlogger*, *ProBlogger*, *CopyBlogger* and *Social Triggers* - who have millions of followers and generate 7-8 figures a year, than trying to find to your own way and getting lost - and later frustrated - in the process.

By spending an hour now reading this book and applying the principles taught here, you will save yourself countless hours of frustration and eventually giving up once the first enthusiasm has dissipated.

You obviously have something great to share with the world. But sharing only works if you have an audience. Otherwise, what's the point?

So share! - and make sure that as many people as possible can read your awesome content and enjoy it.

I wish you good luck on that journey - and don't forget to have fun! - It's supposed to be fun first and foremost....;-)

All the very best,

Gundi Gabrielle
SassyZenGirl.com

Chapter 1: Finding a Blog Topic that People Actually Want to Read...

Finding the "right" blog topic is the first big challenge many new bloggers face. I often get emails from readers who have several ideas in mind and can't decide which one to pick, basically asking me to make the decision for them.

Obviously, I cannot do that. It's your blog, your life and has to come from your heart and soul - your passion!

But I can give you a few pointers that will make the decision - and research - a lot easier.

Take some time to review the following 7 steps before making a final decision.

Even if you already know your topic, it might help you to fine tune and narrow down - or get some new ideas.

So here we go:

STEP #1 - The 3 Blog Models

There are basically 3 blog models to choose from:

1) BE an Expert
You know a topic really well and have a wealth of information to share = You ARE an authority on the topic.

2) BORROW Authority
You are interested in or fascinated by a topic, but you are not an expert.

No problem! - Interview others who are or collect what they say/write and distill into lessons. Be clear though about your sources, don't claim them as your own....

3) SHARE while you learn

A very popular model, because people love to be part of an experience. Just think of Reality TV….

You could share how you are trying to learn a new skill or trying to achieve a specific goal like loosing weight, raising money, training your dog etc.
Even travel blogging is sharing an experience - and people obviously love it….

As an example: a man was heavily overweight and set himself a target weight to achieve in 6 months. He started a blog chronicling his journey and grew a huge audience, because people could relate and found his journey inspiring.

He ended up achieving his goal despite many ups and downs, struggles and disappointments - and became a personal trainer a year later….

Needless to say his blog is still thriving.

Ask yourself:

- is there something you always wanted to try or be?

- is there a recurring challenge, problem or fear that you face?

- maybe a challenge you have overcome and can now share as inspiration for others?

- Something that's unique about you or your life?

Can you share that journey?

STEP 2 - Pick a topic people are actually interested in

Should be obvious - but how do you know?

It may surprise you that often the topics *we think* people would be interested in, are not that interesting at all....

Don't assume - be sure!

How?

Several ways:

1) Google your idea plus "forum" and see what comes up. Are there lots of forums? Are they very active? Are people passionate about the topic?

2) Do the same with "blog", plus your topic. Check the results on the first 3 pages of Google and answer the following questions:

Do those blogs have an active audience?

Lots of comments under each post? Lots of social media shares, interactions?

Also, what are the most popular posts on these blogs?

Take some notes. Anything that peaks your interest.

Also, any areas that could be done better, more in-depth? What area has not been explored yet?

In all the above: what problems or frustrations do people share in their comments? And do they get answered adequately?

3) Do the same in related Facebook groups

4) *BuzzSumo.com* - is one of the best resources to research what's trending in any particular field.

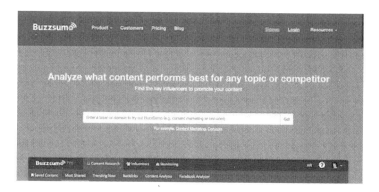

The site lists the most shared articles on any topic for a specific day, week, month or year. You get a good idea of what's trending, how your potential audience "ticks", and also which social media platforms they use.

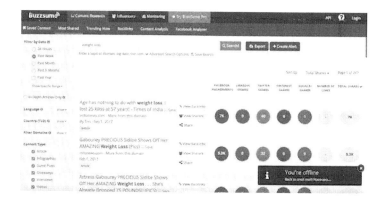

This does not mean you should constantly run after the latest fashion. Not at all. But it is important to understand how people think, what they are interested in - and most of all what they are struggling with! Their challenges, fears, goals, dreams.

If you can help with any of those, your blog will be successful!

Notice that I used the word "help". It will be one of the most important words in your blogging journey and should be at the forefront of any decision, planning or idea you have. The more you can help people, the more they will be drawn to you.

It is really that simple……

5) Use the *Google Keyword Planner* to find out how many monthly searches your niche receives. You will also need this tool for SEO, so it's good to get that set up:

You will need to create an Adwords account, but don't worry, you don't have to run ads. Simply go to *adwords.google.com/ko/KeywordPlanner/* and follow the prompts.

Once your account is set up you can start your

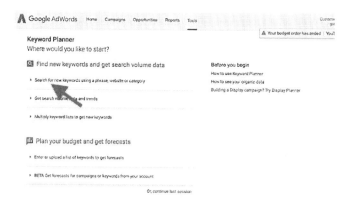

research.

Enter a niche or search term - I used "Budget Travel" in this example - and this window will open:

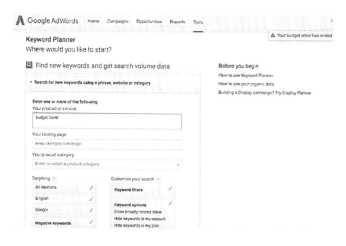

You have a few options to customize your search, though for this purpose I would keep it general and global, unless you are looking to attract a location specific audience.

Then scroll down and click "Get ideas" to open this window with the monthly search results:

Please note that Google no longer gives you exact amounts unless you start an ad campaign, but just the range is sufficient here.

For the overall blog topic you want at least 1000 searches per month, more is better.

By scrolling down further, you can also review related terms and their search volume. Don't pay attention to the "competition" value. That's related to ad campaigns and affiliate products and has nothing to do with "your" blogging competition.

I recommend to spend some time on this step and go through all 5 points. This will give you a good idea whether your target niche has an active, passionate audience and what sub niches to focus on.

STEP 3 - Be passionate

Just like you want a passionate audience, be sure that *you* are passionate about any potential topic.

Blogging isn't always fun. Sometimes you may not be in the mood to write.

Is this something you will still be passionate about 3 or 5 years from now? Passionate enough to write about every week? Research, market etc?

Unless you are 100% sure, don't go there.

It is your passion that will carry you through the drudgery along the way. And it is your passion that will attract people to your blog and keep them engaged.

If you are not passionate, no one else will be…..

STEP 4 - Be specific

This is another important ingredient for your blog success! Rather than writing about an entire niche, pick one particular aspect of that niche. One particular audience group within that niche.

As an example, lets look at the overcrowded niche of travel blogging. Newbies often think, if they just share their daily travel experiences they will naturally draw an audience, but that's too generic and rarely works, beyond just friends and family.

Don't get me wrong, personal experiences are great and you can share those, too. People love them! - Reality Shows and Youtube millionaires are powerful examples.

But if you look closely you will notice that they always have a specific hook - something that's completely unique about them and - they always provide value to their audience. Even if in the form of advice, entertainment or a good laugh.

It is never just about them.

Answer your audience's question of "What's in it for me?" and you are on your way…..

Find out how you can help people and find a specific sub niche / sub audience in that category.

Why?

Because there are millions of general blogs. All with a cute name, all thinking they are unique and interesting - but unfortunately, readers see them as a dime a dozen and quickly move on.

Instead, lets look at a few very successful blogs in the travel niche that have mastered this step to perfection:

Budget Travel: *NomadicMatt.com*
THE resource for budget travel, in part because of his *New York Times* Bestseller, but mostly, because Matt

spent years building an audience around that specific topic. He constantly researches new ways for saving money on travel and that's what people subscribe to.

He also shares his travel experiences and has several destination guides and online courses, but the core of his blog - what he is known for - is how to travel the world for less than $50 a day (the subtitle of his book).

Train Travel: *The Man in Seat 61 - Seat61.com*
THE resource for anything related to train travel. Everybody refers to this site, because it covers every single train trip on planet earth - literally!

It describes the experience, condition of trains, pricing, where to buy tickets etc.
It is the "ultimate" train travel resource.

Asia Travel: *Travelfish.org*
THE resource for anything related to Asia. Detailed destination guides, activities, travel tips, tour companies, pricing etc.

If I need an answer related to Asia travel, I always go to Travelfish first (and I'm not the only one…)

Travel for Women over 40: *GetInTheHotSpot.com*

Obviously…….geared towards female travelers over 40….;-)

Starting a Location Independent Business:
LocationRebel.com

One of THE resource sites for location independence and anyone wanting to become a Digital Nomad and travel indefinitely. Based around one of the top courses in the industry, the blog covers everything related to location independence and online entrepreneurship

While all the above blogs cover a specific sub niche in the travel genre, they still occasionally write about general topics. However, even then, their articles are geared towards their specific audience.

Which brings us to the next step:

STEP 4 - Define your Specific Audience

It's very important to clearly define your audience BEFORE you start your blog!

If you performed the above research, you will have narrowed down several sub niches with enough potential to consistently write about and with a large enough pool of interested readers. Now you want to define your audience - *specifically*.

Spend some picturing who will most likely be drawn to your blog. The comments from forums, Facebook groups and blogs can give you a good indication.

Write a one page description of one specific person within that audience. Doesn't have to be a real person, but be specific about their age, gender, background, profession, interests - and - problems and challenges.

Describe them to a tee and develop a story line.

Blogging is very much like having a conversation with a good friend over a cup of coffee. It is more a chat than an essay and the more you write in this way, the more people will love reading your stuff.

Always talk to ONE specific person, rather than a large group. For the reader it will be as though you are talking to them directly. Intimate and personal - an they will love you for it.

Know their goals, obstacles, challenges and fears - and also what gets them excited and inspired. Write out a story and keep that image in mind when you write.

Talk to that specific person on every single post.

STEP 5 - Distill your topic into 1 sentence - your Tag line

Try to distill what your blog is about into 1 sentence. Spend some time on this and really try to find a slogan/tag line that represents you well.

You will need one - it will be the sub title of your blog and show in your cover picture or logo.

Here are some examples:

NOMADIC MATT: "Travel Better. Cheaper. Longer"

GET IN THE HOT SPOT: "Travel, wellbeing and midlife adventure"

THE PLANET D: "Adventure is for Everyone!"

SASSYZENGIRL: "TRAVEL the World - WORK from Anywhere - LIVE your Dream!"

People who surf the net are in quick mode. They skim through, hoping to find something that either:

* answers their question/solves a problem
- or -
* keeps them engaged/interested/entertained

You only have a few seconds to make your point, and that's why a tag line is so important and something you should keep refining over time.

Don't try too hard to get it "right" the first time. It will probably evolve over time. But start somewhere and keep an open mind.

STEP 6 - Can you monetize your Blog Topic?

If you want to monetize your blog - and why wouldn't you? - research related affiliate products, meaning products that you have tested, ideally use yourself and can now recommend on your blog. You get a commission for helping people finding useful quality products by doing the research for them and writing a review.

To see what products are available in your niche, start with Amazon - one of the biggest affiliate programs in the world - and type your main keyword/niche into their search engine.

Do you see products that you would enjoy marketing and sharing on your blog?

If so, is their price high enough to make a decent commission? Amazon commissions are very low, BUT you get commissions on EVERYTHING that visitor buys within 24 hours of using your link!

When you become an affiliate you get a special link with your ID. Whenever someone clicks on that link, a cookie is installed on their browser. That's how the

affiliate program keeps track on where the sale came from and can then pay you a commission.

Affiliate Marketing will be an entire book in itself, but these are some basics to get you started.

Other affiliate programs include *Clickbank, Commission Junction, Udemy* (for courses) and countless company associated programs.

Whenever you like a company or product, google the name plus "affiliate" and see if there is an affiliate program you can sign up for.

You can then place a link into a blog article, usually a product review, or a banner in your side bar, footer, inline etc.

Give it a try. Can you find affiliate products in your niche that you can relate to and could market?

Quality products that you are excited about and could full heartedly recommend?

STEP 7 - Final Test

Now that you have narrowed down your ideas to just a few, ask yourself:

- Can you generate 30 article ideas? Try! - Set yourself 20 minutes and see what you can come up with. Don't get hung up on the number. You will know as you do this little exercise, whether this is a topic you can extensively write about long term.

- What is unique about your idea that is not covered anywhere else. How can YOU do better? What has been missing so far?

- Do you get excited just thinking about it? Can't wait to start writing?

- What is your hook?

And write down the answers to each questions.

Then take a day or two, don't think about it and let it sit. If after 2-3 days you are still just as excited, you are ready to go!

In the meantime you can start with the other chapters of this book and learn how to write blogging style and how to draw an audience to your blog....

Chapter 2 - How to Find Viral Blog Post Ideas

Always be aware of current trends in your field. You don't have to follow every fashion, but at least occasionally, once a month in the beginning, find a topic that has gone viral recently and put your own twist on it.

Find another angle that is missing, a sub point that could use further exploring. Maybe you noticed during your research from Chapter 1 certain problems or difficulties that haven't been properly answered yet where you can add value and go more in-depth. Add something unique.

How do you find trending topics?

Your two best resources are:

1) The top blogs in your niche

Subscribe to at least 10 and pay attention to what they are writing about and what their most popular posts have been over the past few months. You can also follow them on Twitter or Facebook and see what other content (articles from other sources) they share.

Top bloggers usually spend a good amount of time researching their audience's interests, so in the beginning it's helpful to follow their lead and see what they focus on.

Not for every post you write, obviously. Otherwise, you are just a carbon copy of someone else, but once a month.

Over time you will get a sense of what works and also what your audience is responding to. But even top bloggers still subscribe and follow other blogs to remain aware of what's going on in their scene. You never stop learning and improving.

2) BuzzSumo.com

Make it a habit to check once a week on a sub topic in your niche, or your niche in general and see what comes up.

BuzzSumo shows you the most shared posts on any topic during the last day, week, month, year etc, so mix it up a little.

Once you find something that seems interesting, read the post and see how you can improve and give it your own take.

Also, do a google search on forums and blogs for the same topic and read comments to see where people still have questions or problems and incorporate that into your post.

Take note of the blogs that come up on page 1 in Google - and on *BuzzSumo*. This can be a great opportunity to network with bigger blogs and their audience.

Don't see them as competition. Quite the opposite - they can be your greatest ally in the beginning.

Once your post is finished, send them an email, briefly introduce yourself, mention how you liked their post and what *specifically* helped you/inspired you - and then let them know that you added some additional information/resources in your own recent post.

They might actually share your article with their readership - or share on social media - and that can be a great jump starter for your blog.

Influencers always look for interesting content to share with their audience, especially on social media, so don't be shy or think you have to be well known first.

As long as you keep it brief, have value to offer (don't ask for their "help") and write well (more on that in the next chapter), you will find influencers willing to share your content.

More on how to approach them in the traffic generation chapter.

How to schedule?

To make all this less overwhelming, take a weekend, spend some time on the above research and then design a post schedule for the next 4 weeks.

1 post per week is enough, but try to get into that regular weekly rhythm.

Make it a mix of shorter posts on topics that are important to you and/or experiences you want to share, and at least one trending, more in-depth post per month (1000+ words, more is better).

In-depth, "ultimate guide" type posts do really well, but, of course, you can't do those every week.

You will find a rhythm over time of what works for you and your audience. Just start somewhere and adjust along the way.

One word of caution:

Obviously, NEVER copy someone else's work. Not just for ethical and legal reasons, but also to avoid a "duplicate content" penalty from Google who would consider such copies spam (trust me, you don't ever want a google penalty…..more on that in the SEO book).

It is ok to quote a sentence here and there, but make it clear who the source is and ideally link back to that source.

Otherwise, you can take a general idea and rewrite it. But always try to add something unique and of value.

Once you have an audience - even a small one - ask them occasionally what they would like to hear about. What problems, challenges they face that you might provide an answer to.

Over time, they will become your best resource. And the more you provide helpful content, the more they will recommend you and share you = free publicity…..

Chapter 3 - The Writing Style of Blogging

The next ingredient to a successful blog is learning the writing style of blogging - and learn it well!

Yes, you could just write and hope for the best. Maybe you are even an English or journalism major and feel you "got" this.

Think again.

Writing to a blogging audience is completely different from any other writing you have ever done.

Blogging is more like a conversation with a good friend over a cup of coffee.

It's conversational, fun, hip. Not always full sentences or grammatically perfect. More like you would talk, rather than write.

It's not about writing a great work of literature or a scientific paper - though the writing should still be good, of course, - but more like chatting with a friend.

To see the difference, record a conversation with a friend once where you passionately share something with them. You know a lot, you are totally into it. You are inspired, passionate, knowledgable - and you have a point to make!

Then write a transcript of that recording - and read it.

That's very much what blogging is like!

Unless it's fun to read and engaging you are missing the point.

Even when you are writing about a serious issue - still have a conversation with your reader (the specific person you described in chapter 1), rather than giving them a lecture or writing an essay.

Otherwise, they'll leave quickly!

Think about how you are reading articles on the internet.

Very different from reading a book!

Usually, you are searching for something - some answer or advice. You are in quick mode.

You google a keyword and scan through the results. You click on a few, scan the page and decide within seconds whether you stay or move on.

Keep that in mind - also in your visual design:

Use large fonts that are easy to read. A dark font color. Enough white background space to not feel crowded. Colored or dark backgrounds usually don't work well, so don't be too creative in the beginning.

Better a simple, clean design that's easy to read than a complicated font and too much color.

Again, watch yourself next time. Do you stay on a page that feels cramped, with tiny text and dark background?

Do you even care much about the design if you just want some information?

I'll leave the answer to you…..

From now on, whenever you google something, pay attention to your search mode. How do you decide? What keeps you engaged? What do you like about certain sites and not others? And then apply those observations to your blog.

This is another reason not to spend too much time in the beginning with complex designs and features. Rather focus on good content and learning the basics and add the rest later.

Your blog design should be pleasant, easy to read and scan over. Uncrowded, clean.

How to engage potential readers?

#1 - CAPTIVATING HEADLINES

One of the most important factors to draw people to your site!

Again, think of what headlines you respond to and watch those from now on. Analyze the headlines that draw you in, that you just *have* to read? - What was it that made them so irresistible? And do you see patterns that work again and again?

You will learn so much from just doing that.

There is a science to effective headlines and you can easily learn it. Just use tested templates in the beginning. Those that haven proven to work well and draw readers in.

The two most popular headline templates are:

* The List Post
* The "How to" Post

An example for a list post would be "5 Tips to do loose weight after the holidays" or "The 10 Best Resorts for families in Florida".

"How to" are self-explanatory and are almost as frequent as list posts.

You see both templates everywhere.

Why?

Because they work!

And why do they work so well?

Because it *seems* much easier and faster to read through a list of points than large chunks of texts.

It's an illusion, of course, because list posts can be just as long, but they *feel* shorter.

The appeal of "How to" posts is obvious: Most of the time when we google we are looking for instructions or explanations of some sort - and that's exactly what "how to" posts provide.

They answer a question, hopefully in an easy-to-understand, simple way - at least that's what we hope for.

For a more complete list of effective headline templates covering all kinds of different situations, I recommend ***Jon Morrow's Headline Hacks.*** For free access, just click this link:

It will be one of the most important things you will ever download.

Jon is one of the most successful bloggers in the world and makes 7 figures from just his current blog alone - definitely someone I would listen to. He also has a really interesting life story - and….. he is paralyzed from the neck down….

#2 - SHORT PARAGRAPHS

I see many posts with really long paragraphs making them difficult to read. Often with tiny font and not enough line spacing - or a curly font that's hard to decipher.

Again, make it pleasant and easy to read. 1-2 sentences per paragraph and have a large enough font size. White background, uncrowded.

Also, break it up with sub heads - H2s as they are called. Makes it so much easier to read and scan through.

This is how you format them:

Highlight the text you want to turn into a sub head and then go to "paragraph -> Heading 2"

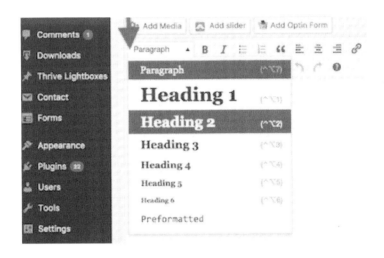

#3 - OPENING HOOK

Your first line will usually determine whether someone stays on your article or clicks the back button, so be sure to get that one right.

You need to connect with people emotionally and draw them in. If you master that - and anyone can learn this - you will be a lot more successful.

To illustrate the above 3 points, let me share a few examples.

I'm using guest articles I wrote a while back that were published on top blogs with large and engaged audiences. All received lots of shares and comments:

* **Goodlife Zen:**
GoodLifeZen.com/Transform-Anger-Into-Joy/

* Headline

I'm sure you noticed, this is a classic list post - and yet it's not a short article (2000+ words).

5 POWERFUL WAYS TO TRANSFORM ANGER INTO JOY

Compare this headline with "Helpful Tips to Control Your Anger" - or similar.

What seems easier to read?

Obviously, the list post. It seems short and concise. Something that even with a busy schedule I can digest quickly. It's only 5 "ways" after all.

Next, notice the "power words":

Powerful
Transform
Anger
Joy

Power words invoke the reader's emotion and draw them in. Always have a least 1-2 in your headlines and sprinkle some throughout the text. Here is an extensive list of power words:

SumoMe.com/Stories/Power-Words

* Opening Hook

Have a look at the opening line:

"It happened again."

Whether or not you are interested in this article, you will be curious about: **what** happened again?

It also feels like something that could happen again to *you*. You are hooked and you want to know more.

And…… now you already stayed longer than 5 seconds, which is what we were aiming for.

The 2nd paragraph goes even further.

"You tried to stop yourself. You wished you hadn't said it. And yet, despite all your best efforts, you lost it once again."

Anyone who has ever been angry or has an anger problem, can relate!

With the first 2-3 paragraphs you show people that you understand how they _feel_ and where they are coming from. Once you connect in that way, they will be a lot more willing to listen and read more.

* Paragraphs & Sub Heads

If you look further through the whole article, you will notice that paragraphs are short and H2s frequent.

This helps to scan through quickly if you aren't sure yet or don't have much time. If the H2s catch your attention, you might read the full article or at least full sections.

If on the other hand, there is just a large block of text with no sub heads, you will most likely click the back button and look elsewhere.

Watch yourself next time when you google something....

GUEST BLOGGING

While we are on the topic - Guest Blogging is one of THE most effective ways to attract an audience.

It is the fastest way to build a following in the beginning, because you are leveraging someone else's audience that was built over years.

And it's not just traffic you are attracting....

Let me share the amazing opportunities that came from another guest post:

The Planet D

ThePlanetD.com/Walk-With-Cheetahs-Conservation-Africa/

I'm a travel writer and *The Planet D* is the biggest travel blog in the world with millions of followers.

I wrote the above article a while back and soon after was traveling in Australia. Lo and behold, *Great Southern Rail* who love *The Planet D* saw my article and invited me onto their legendary luxury train - the *Indian Pacific* - from Perth to Sydney. A 4 day journey with my own cabin, all inclusive, a $3000 value - all because of exposure I got from one guest post!

You may think I'm a well-trained writer with years of experience and college training - but I'm not! - I'm a classical musician and had no writing experience at all when I first started!

Yet, I'm now a multiple bestselling author, run a large travel blog, and easily got accepted by some of the top blogs in the business.

The reason is simple: I spent time in the beginning to learn how to write well - and it wasn't all that time consuming - nor was it expensive!

I learned from the top writers in the business and applied their methods and techniques.

Within weeks of finishing the initial course, I was accepted by 3 major blogs!

Of course, you never finish learning, it's a constant work in progress - but the groundwork was laid and that's one of the most important things you can do for your blogging career.

It's the one area you canNOT skip! - or you will never get far and be stuck with just a few hundred readers, if that.

The course I did was a **guest blogging course by Jon Morrow** who at one point was the highest paid writer on the internet with $7,000 per article!

You can check it out here:

SassyZenGirl.com/Guest-Blogging

As I mentioned before, Jon achieved this tremendous success despite being completely paralyzed from the neck down.

The course does not just teach you how to land high level guest blogging gigs - incl. a little Black Book with direct editor emails for over 100 top blogs, incl. the *Huffington Post, Lifehack*, and *Forbes* - but more importantly, it teaches you **how to write** - blogging style.

How to engage an audience and draw them in, what headlines to use etc.

Best of all, once you complete the course - which can easily be done in 4 weeks at your own pace - you can mention in your pitch that you passed Jon's course, and the editors, who all know him, will then be much more willing to give you a chance, since you have been properly trained and know what they expect and need to see in a post.

They are not taking as much of a chance as they would with a complete newbie, and the traffic you can get from just a few high powered guest posts is tremendous and can jump start your blog.

Here is another example. This is a more experiential post, but follows the same principles:

ADaringAdventure.com/Gifts-From-Nelson-Mandela/

Another list post, power words in the title and look at the opening line:

"It isn't often that I get as deeply moved….."

No matter what the title or topic, an opening like this draws people in. We all *love* to be deeply moved and most readers will go at least a little further to find out if *they* can be deeply moved as well

Always remember the "what's in it for me?" mentality of your readers.

Looking at the first two paragraphs, notice some more evocative power words:

"Notorious", "infamous", "gift" - and once again, "powerful" and "transformative", all adding intrigue to an already fascinating topic.

This article received almost 5000(!) shares and numerous emails and comments. People were clearly moved. It touched something in them, and the first line drew them in.

Of course, it didn't hurt to have a well known blogger like Tim Brownson, owner of "A Daring Adventure", writing this intro:

I'm not sharing this to brag, not at all - but to show you that it's really not that difficult and you don't need months and years of training or spend hundreds or thousands of dollars.

This was only my 3rd guest post, written a few weeks after completing Jon's course - and this is the response I got....

If I can do it, so can you!

Anatomy of a Perfect Blog Post

Derek Halpern, another highly successful blogger and internet entrepreneur published this visual graph to illustrate a "perfect" blog structure.

SocialTriggers.com/Perfect-Blog-Post/

You might want to print this out and check your future articles against it. Obviously, you don't need to follow every single detail and some parts will work better in some niches than others, but it's a good overall structure to go by.

And here is a **Simple Blog Post Blue Print**:

- **Headline**
- **Opening Hook** describing a common problem. Relate to how the reader *feels*.
- **Promise a Solution**
- **Provide a Solution**
  The bulk of the article with lots of sub points/H2s
- **Conclusion**

More Popular Post Types

In addition to *List posts* and *How to posts*, these are a few more popular blog post templates:

* Ultimate Resource Post
an in-depth article covering a topic completely with lots of graphs, screenshots, videos, resources etc.

* Case Study
Follow along your experiences, how you applied a certain technique - or chronicle someone else's

* Serialized Articles

* Influential People Post
Refer to a quote or article from an influencer/celebrity and share your personal experiences on how this helped/inspired you.

Be sure to mention their name in the headline. It's always a huge draw even if people don't like that person.

If you can, interview them, either live or on paper - and include an unexpected question (example: "when does Tim Ferris work more than 4 hours")

Review Posts
Always popular, especially for affiliate products.

Comparison Posts
Similar to review posts, except you compare 2 or 3 items, courses, movies, books etc.

Survey your Readers
Free Wordpress plugins like *Survey Monkey* and *WP Polls* allow you to conduct surveys directly with your readers. A GREAT way to engage an audience and a wonderful basis for your next article.

Chapter 4 - How to Drive Traffic to Your Blog

Now lets look at methods to draw people to your blog - and not just any people, but those who actually want to read what you have to say!

The 3 main strategies most books will talk about are:

Social Media Marketing
SEO = *Search Engine Optimization, e.g. how to rank high in Google*
Guest Blogging

I would also include **Kindle publishing** which has been a great way for me to introduce new readers to my blog and build a list.

Social Media, SEO and Kindle Publishing all take a little time to show results and are described in the next 3 books of this series.

In this chapter, let's look at 10 simple strategies that you can implement right now:

#1 - Submit to Share services like Quuu, Viral Content Bee and Triberr

- **Quuu**.com is a paid service that allows you to submit you best blog posts for review to Quuu's well-trained editorial staff. They manually read every submission and only approve well written and informative content. If your article gets approved it will be made available to thousands bloggers and business owners who constantly need good content for their social media marketing. It's a great and easy way to spread an awesome article to a wide audience and the manual review system ensures that only quality content will be shared.

- **ViralContentBee**.com offers free and paid plans to promote your content across social media. With the free version you earn credits every time you share someone else's content on your own social media platforms. VCB's team manually checks that everyone's social media profiles are real and active with regularly updated content and audience interaction (retweets, likes, comments) to keep spammers out.

- **Triberr**.com is another free platform that allows you to join "Tribes" of like-minded bloggers who share each other's content on social media, as well as comment and like. Triberr has hundreds of thousands of members, incl. Influential bloggers and is another great way to spread your content to a wide audience.

#1 - Guest Blogging

I know I am repeating myself, but when you are starting out, there is really no other technique that can jump start your blog as quickly as guest blogging.

Every successful blogger started that way. It is THE most important thing you can do in the beginning.

Of course, this only works if you guest post on blogs with a large following and an active audience, e.g. lots of comments, social media shares etc. And - if the blog allows you to place a short bio at the end with a backlink to your site, so people can find you.

Be sure to check on ALL the above before offering a guest post.

If you want success quickly, I recommend signing up for Jon's training. Not only do you learn good blogging style, headlines and how to pitch your ideas to potential bloggers and editors, but it also comes with a "Little Black Book" of direct editor contacts from 100+ thoroughly vetted blogs - many of them quite famous - who will be much more open to reading your stuff if you come through this training.

Sign up here:

SassyZenGirl.com/Guest-Blogging

And here is a great article explaining the submission requirements for top blogs like Forbes, Entrepreneur & Business Insider:

AuthorityAlchemy.com/Become-a-Contributor-for-Forbes/

#3 - "Boost" your Posts with Facebook Ads

This is easy and inexpensive to do. You need a Facebook fan page and then you share your blog post on that page.

This video shows you how to set up a "boost" and choose the right target audience:

SassyZenGirl.com/Boost-Facebook-Ads

#4 - Share a Quiz

A quiz related to your blog topic is a fun way to engage an audience. People LOVE them and will often share their results on social media, giving you additional great exposure.

Quizzes are easy to set up. There are plugins that do most of the heavy lifting and a great one I've used is
Thrive Quiz Builder:
SassyZenGirl.com/Thrive-Quiz-Builder

#5 - Run Contests and Giveaways

Another audience favorite and a great way to attract new readers. This article shows you how to set it up.:

Shoutmeloud.com/how-a-free-blog-contest-will-help-your-blog.html

#6 - Build Relationships with Top Bloggers/ Influencers in your Field

This is a big one! - And it goes beyond just guest blogging. Networking with the top bloggers in your field is one of the most important things you can do while building your blog.

Don't see them as competition. To succeed you need a solid network of fellow bloggers, and you can all help each other.

Obviously, top bloggers are very busy and won't just respond because you wrote to them. You need to build relationships over time.

Here is how:

First, identify 10 top blogs in your field. Spend a few days on this, read their blogs, see who you connect with best, whose style you really like.

Read all their "most popular" posts and also read the comments underneath.

How are they writing and structuring their posts? What do they cover well and where do you see room for improvement, an opportunity for you to add value?

What can you learn from the comments? - What questions do people ask and might you have an answer or advice for them?

Very important: Leave comments underneath each post! Something you *specifically* like or ask a question - and be sure to have a **Gravatar** with your photo.

Go to ***Gravatar.com*** for set up.

You can also include your website when filling out the comment form, so others can find you, plus, you get a backlink to your blog (important for SEO, even if forum links are not very powerful, they certainly never hurt).

Once you found 10 top blogs you like, subscribe to all of them and whenever they have a new post, be sure to read and leave a comment. Once again, be specific. Have something interesting to say or ask a question, not just "great post".

Over time, the blogger will notice you. Usually, they will reply, so this is a great way to get on their radar.

If you see someone ask a question and you have a good answer, reply to that comment. You are helping the blogger who often has a LOT of comments and emails to reply to and people will start noticing you.

Be VERY sure though, to NOT promote your blog in any way - it's SO annoying and your comment will most likely get deleted. Instead, add value. Either a good comment or a helpful answer.

Also share their posts on your social media and be sure to tag them, so they know.

If applicable, use one of their quotes in a blog post and tweet at them. If you have a great article, they might retweet it to their huge audience. If even one major blogger does that, the impact can be tremendous.

Whenever you link out to one of their posts in your articles - in other words, whenever you are sending them free traffic - you can let them know. Not every single time, obviously, but when you are writing them anyway, it's a nice additional thing to mention - or to start the conversation with.

Always look out for opportunities to add value through a new post. Maybe something is missing or you can cover a part in much greater detail that would complement the original post without "competing".

Once you find something, write a post. Fine tune it, apply all the principles from chapter 3, and when you feel ready, write a short email to the blogger.

Don't ask for help. Remember successful bloggers often get hundreds of emails per week. Be brief, introduce yourself and mention how one of their posts *specifically* helped you or inspired you.

Then mention that you covered an additional aspect in a recent article that might be of interest to their readers and suggest they share it.

That's it.

If you indeed add value and the post is well written, there is a good chance that they are interested in sharing - and you are getting free traffic to your blog!

A little trick to get their attention faster is subscribing to their email list and then reply to a message they sent.

They will be much more likely to respond when they see their own subject line and know you are an active reader of their blog, than someone who is just begging for a favor (which is what most people do).

If you don't have an article yet, you can also ask a one part question that can easily be answered in a minute or two. Be sure to offer some value in return, like promising to share their content with your followers or on social media.

Again, be mindful that bloggers are usually very busy, and it may take a while until they get back to you.

Never be pushy or disappointed if you don't get an enthusiastic response. Think how you would see an email like yours if you received several hundred each week……

Keep it simple, be respectful of their time and keep posting comments and sharing their content. Eventually, you might be able to ask for a guest post - maybe even a Skype call, if there is a good enough reason (like you interviewing them on a relevant topic and posting it on your blog).

But mostly, give it time. Let the relationship grow naturally and with enough breathing room for both sides.

#7 - Comment in Forums and Facebook Groups

This one is obvious, but once again don't start by marketing your blog or posts. It's really annoying and can even get you banned.

Instead, participate in the conversation. Answer questions, be helpful wherever you can, and people will start noticing you.

Then, when you see a question or problem that requires a more in-depth explanation, you can write a short blog post and add it in your reply for further reading. By that time, people know you as someone who knows their stuff and isn't just there for selfish reasons. They will then be quite interested in reading a post of yours and it doesn't feel like spam.

Again - and I can't say this often enough - reading comments on a regular basis will *also* give you great ideas for future posts and even ebooks - plus, it's a wonderful networking opportunity.

So, start establishing authority in related forums and Facebook groups. Give value first, answer questions and help people. Then - occasionally - share a relevant article. The emphasis being on *occasionally*. Don't spam! - It's annoying!

#8 - Include Click-to-Tweets in your Posts

Click to Tweet is a great *Wordpress* plugin that encourages readers to tweet a phrase or quote from your post.

> Tweetable quotes are a simple and elegant way to bring more traffic from Twitter http://ctt.ec/n6oH1+ @nickchurick
>
> ──────────▶ CLICK TO TWEET

Include tweet-able quotes or catchphrases - an actionable piece of advice - and place 1 or 2 throughout your article.

This is what it looks like - placed somewhere within your text:

A "Click To Tweet" is a great example of a "Call to Action" or "CTA". It's a marketing term and will be one of the most important words in your blogging career.

Whenever you want people to do something - be it sign up to your blog, buy something, share your post or comment - you need to tell them.

I know it sounds strange, but don't assume people know or will do it automatically. Most of the time they won't, but if you ask they are often more than happy to comply.

#9 - StumbleUpon

StumbleUpon is a discovery search engine that allows users to rate and recommend articles and videos. Once an article has been "stumbled", it goes into a line up and will be seen by more viewers with similar interests. If the article keeps getting high ratings, it can become a snowball effect and even go viral.

The opposite is also true when a post gets mostly thumbs down - so only use quality content for this.

StumbleUpon is a browser extension and can be set up at: *StumbleUpon.com* or through your social media share bar.

For some awesome strategies to get huge traffic from *StumbleUpon* check out this article:

Blog.Kissmetrics.com/Increase-Traffic-With-Stumbleupon/

#10 - Social Media Share Bar

Obviously, you should have a social media share bar on your blog, and ideally a floating one that moves as visitors scroll down while reading an article.

A great - free - Floating Bar with many additional features is **SumoMe** (sumome.com). You can add it directly from within your *WordPress* Admin area.

Chapter 5 - How to Convert Traffic into Subscribers

Driving traffic to your blog is useless, unless you convert that traffic into subscribers - or at the very least, social media followers.

How to convert?

Well, aside from compelling content that people really want to read - which will always be the most important factor - you need to make it easy for people to sign up to your mailing list/newsletter.

In other words, you need a sign up form on your blog - ideally several in different places.

Where to place a sign up form?

Extensive testing by professional marketers has shown the following areas on a website to have the highest conversion rate:

1) **Top of your side bar**. You absolutely need one there and right underneath you can add your social media icons.

2) **End of each post**. Another very effective area. After all, someone just read your whole article, so they are obviously interested. Make it easy for them to stay in touch.

3) **Footer** or **Header**. *Hello Bar* and *Viper Bar* are great free plugins for header forms. They are very effective, because the form always shows at the top of your page, so it's quite tempting.

4) **Pop ups** are annoying, yes, but their conversion rate is amazing, which is why everybody uses them. You don't need them right from the start, but consider adding them later, especially if conversion of your other forms is not great.

5) Finally, one of *the* most effective places to have a sign up form is a **Feature box** at the top of your home page, overlapping your cover picture. More on that in a moment…..

How to design a sign up form?

To keep it simple, just start with a side bar and inline form. That's all you really need in the beginning.

A free and easy tool to set this up is "Optin Cat".

It's a *Wordpress* plugin and the free version is all you need.

You can choose from 2 styles for both side bar and inline form and easily format them with your colors, fonts, styles etc.

You will then need to connect that form with a mailing list service. Two good options are *AWeber* and *Mail-chimp*.

Mail-chimp starts with a free version for the first 2000 subscribers, but it comes with a number of limitations (no autoresponder etc.). It's a good provider though and if you don't want to spend money initially, just start with that.

Whatever provider you choose, you will first need to set up your account and then connect with your *Optin Cat* form from within your *Wordpress* Admin area. (Same goes for contact forms, btw)

Youtube offers numerous video tutorials as do the mailing list providers - and you can even ask their tech support to set it up for you. It can be a bit confusing in the beginning.

Be sure to test the whole sequence several times to make sure all steps are in place.

What to write in your optin form?

Always provide a "freebie" to entice people to subscribe. Just asking to "subscribe to the newsletter" is usually not enough to hook people in, unless they are already absolutely in love with your blog.

A freebie can be a free report or ebook or a free email course that you send over several days (for that you would need an autoresponder feature from your mailing list provider).

It *has* to be something useful to the reader. Something they would really want and are willing to give their email address for.

Think about an awesome tip or instruction you can give, that's not easily available anywhere else and turn it into a free report. Doesn't have to be long, but it *has* to be important to the reader - and of course, should have a great, attention grabbing headline (see chapter 3).

Save it as a pdf and use *WP Download Manager* plugin - or - even simpler, write the report on a blog page (not a "post", as that would show in your blog feed). As long as the page url is not publicly available, you are getting the same effect.

Then offer that "freebie" on your sign up form and set up the sequence.

Here are some examples:

Side bar sign up form:

Feature Box sign up form right on the cover photo:

Inline sign up form at the end of each article:

Be sure to have an attention grabbing headline and an interesting text on your button. Not just "sign up" or "subscribe".

Humor is always great. "Gimme" works well, or something else that's cool and interesting.

From now on, pay close attention to sign up forms whenever you see them. You will quickly notice which are appealing to you and which make you run the other way - and also what freebies other bloggers offer and how effective you find them…..

Chapter 6 - How to Make Money with Your Blog

You have 3 main options to monetize your blog:

#1 - Affiliate marketing = sell someone else's products

#2 - Sell your own products: books, courses, merchandise, services

#3 - Sell ad space

#3 applies once you have a significant following and companies will contact you automatically when you reach that level. Payout is usually not very high, so I wouldn't focus too much on that for now.
If you want to check it out though, the company that is frequently recommended among bloggers is **Mediavine.com**.

Here is some more food for thought on this subject as shared by some of the top blogs:

13 Reasons Why Blog Ads Suck For Monetizing Your Site
smartblogger.com/blog-ads/

Don't Put Ads On Your Blog
www.blogtyrant.com/dont-put-ads-on-your-blog/

Can Bloggers Make Money Without Google Adsense
www.shoutmeloud.com/life-after-google-adsense.html

#1 and 2 can be great sources of passive income and you can start right away.

#1 Affiliate Marketing

We briefly touched on this option in chapter 1. You recommend products on your blog and receive a commission whenever someone buys. A great source of passive income when set up right.

First, you want to find products in your niche that you are excited to promote - ideally products you use yourself.

As mentioned in chapter 1, a great place to start is *Amazon*. Just go to their site and put in keywords related to your niche and see what comes up.

Are there any products you are genuinely excited about that you could see yourself recommending? Are their prices high enough to earn you a decent commission?

What do the reviews say? (very important)

Once you find a few, I would recommend buying the product and testing it out for yourself. Then write a review post, describing all the pros and cons and include your affiliate link.

First, of course, you need to sign up with *Amazon*'s Affiliate Program and then get a "hop-link" for each product. That's a url with your particular affiliate ID. Whenever someone clicks on it, a cookie will be installed on that person's browser and anything that person buys on Amazon within 24 hours will earn you a commission! - not just the product you are recommending!

This is great, though keep in mind that *Amazon*'s commission rate is overall very low and their rules are extremely strict. Violate them even once and your account gets banned forever.

This is one time when you really need to read the full affiliate agreement and make sure you take note of every single rule.

Other well known affiliate programs are *Clickbank, Commission Junction, Udemy* (for courses) and countless company owned programs or online courses.

You can also google your niche and the word "affiliate program" or a specific product you like with "affiliate Program" and see what you can promote.

In the beginning, I would pick 2 or 3, start with review posts and put a banner in the side bar or somewhere within your blog text.

Be sure to pick quality products you can *full heartedly* recommend. People will trust your judgement and recommendation, so make sure to honor that trust.

My friend Julia created a nice Affiliate Beginner Course. She is a stay-at-home Mom from Canada and built a 6 figure income from affiliate marketing over the years. She agreed to give SassyZenGirl readers a massive discount. Instead of $49.95, you can grab the course for just $19.95 by adding coupon code SAVENOW at checkout.

Grab it HERE:
SassyZenGirl.com/Affiliate-Course

#2 Sell your own Products

This can be anything from online courses, ebooks, merchandise, services etc. You can even combine your blog with an eCommerce store.

Course creation is a whole extensive topic of its own and can be a great way to create long term passive income.

But even if you don't have a course yet, you can use your blog to start building a list that you can later market your courses to. It will be much easier to market to a group of people that already trust you than selling cold. And, of course, do it sparingly or people will start unsubscribing...

An easier and rather quick way to create a sellable product is an ebook - or series of ebooks.

An ebook can start with 10,000 words and can also be used as a freebie/sign up incentive.

A great way to market ebooks and drive traffic to your site is obviously Kindle Publishing and the 5th book in this series goes into detail on how to do just that.

Even without Kindle though, you can create a simple ebook in pdf format and make it available as a download on your blog. To collect payment, PayPal is usually a good and safe option - and pretty easy to set up.

The same goes for any other products you have to offer and, of course, for any services or consulting you can provide.

Once again - a blog can be a great way to build a list of loyal readers AND ALSO of potential customers for your products and services - never lose sight of that awesome potential a blog offers.

BONUS Chapter: Travel Blogging

As a bonus, this video and article will give you a better sense of how travel blogging works and whether it could be a good fit for you.

SassyZenGirl.com/Become-Travel-Blogger

The first part covers general blogging topics that you already know from this book, but then goes further into the skills specific to travel blogging:

* Networking with travel outfits
* Building partnerships with sponsors
* Getting invited on press trips
* Free hotel stays/tours

and much more……

Final Words

There you have it!

I hope this little book gave you some ideas on how to plan the next steps for your long term blogging success.

All new ventures can be a little scary in the beginning, because you don't know what's going to happen - and starting a blog is no different.

In case you are worried, just remember, everyone makes mistakes. They are part of the game and you WILL definitely make some - even the most successful bloggers do.

I love how the great inventor Thomas Edison viewed failure and mistakes:

"I have not failed. I've just found 10,000 ways that won't work."

Awesome!

Successful people usually make a lot MORE mistakes, because they stick with their goal, no matter what. Just keep going, be flexible and adjust direction (and even the niche/topic) if needed and you will get there.

The worst that can happen is you wasted a little time. But is it really wasted?

Probably not, because of the experience you gained and everything you learned from it. You can then leverage all that to get even better!

Have a long term mind set

Blogging success doesn't usually come overnight. It takes time to build a following and find a rhythm that works for you.

You need a long term mind set and don't be disappointed if things don't work right away. They often don't.

You are now way ahead of the game, because you know what it takes to be a successful blogger and what steps to cover next. 95% of new bloggers never learn those.

The rest is just applying what you learned - and *keep* applying until you are successful.

"Rinse and repeat" as they say…..

One more important ingredient:

Definitely, get your own web hosting! - Don't waste precious time on amateur platforms like *Weebly*, *Blogger* or *WordpressCOM* (different from the non-profit **Wordpress.org** software that all successful bloggers use).

Only then, will you have complete control over your content. And only then will you have access to thousands of free, amazing plugins and tools to make your blog more successful and functional.

A "free" blog may be tempting initially, but you will soon find that it isn't really free and that the limitations will force you to switch to one of their paid programs - or move to *Wordpress.org* altogether.

Eventually, you'll have to move anyway, and by then it will be much more complicated. You will probably have to hire someone to transfer your blog and all its content. And you might lose your domain name....

If you took the extra effort of reading this book, don't be skimpy on $3.49/per month for quality hosting when it means having complete control over your blog and content and a MUCH wider range of tools (free plugins/apps) that will not work with the cheap freebie sites.

You can start by **registering a domain name** and then find a good, reliable hosting company.

If you want a big discount (56%) on one of the Top rated hosting services, click this link:

SassyZenGirl.com/Web-Hosting

Or do your own research to find a suitable company.

Just don't waste your precious time and resources on commercial blogging platforms. You will regret it in the long run!

Finally….

Start today!

Don't just move on to the next ebook or course. Get a notebook and go back to the beginning of this book and read again - this time, applying the steps outlined here.

Take consistent action and watch your blog grow! - It's fun and such an amazing feeling when you suddenly communicate with people from all around the world who are excited to read your stuff and follow your blogging journey!

Support and Networking Group

If you have any questions, would like feedback on your blog/ website or social media strategy - or - would like to network with other budding bloggers, authors, and entrepreneurs, come and join us in the brand new SassyZenGirl Support & Networking Facebook Group. It's a fun, friendly and supportive environment where you can share your projects and network with others.

Join HERE:
Facebook.com/Groups/SassyZenGirl

I wish you all the best & much success and fulfillment!

Happy Blogging!

Gundi Gabrielle
SassyZenGirl.com

Interested in FREE Books?

Then join the Launch Team and get all my current and future books for free.

As a test reader & reviewer, you will have access to a free review copy of each book you are interested in reading (ebook format). You can choose which books and topics you want to review.

How to apply?

Please send a message with the following information to **contact@SassyZenGirl.com**:

- Link to your Amazon review of this book

- Which of my books have you read so far?

- Can you commit to reading a book within 1 week and give feedback?

- Are you interested in travel or business / internet marketing - or both?

Anything else you'd like to share….

More SassyZenGirl Books:

#1 Bestselling
BEGINNER INTERNET MARKETING
Series

TRAVEL for FREE

How to score FREE
Flights, Rental Cars & Accommodations,
dramatically reduce Airfares,
Get paid to Travel &
START a DIGITAL NOMAD BIZ
you can run from anywhere
in the world!

About the Author

Gundi Gabrielle is a 8-time #1 Bestselling Author, Internet Entrepreneur and Digital Nomad.

A former Carnegie Hall conductor and Concert Organist, she decided 3 years ago to make a bold change in her life, packed up a few belongings and drove all the way from Santa Monica, California, to Alaska. She has been traveling ever since and loves exploring this beautiful world without being tied to one place.

She has road tripped through all 50 US States and parts of Canada, lived in several European countries for a number of years and visited most of Europe, as well South America, Southern Africa, Australia, New Zealand and many countries in South East Asia and the Middle East.

She runs the Travel Blog *SassyZenGirl*, writes travel and blogging books and often house or farm sits along her travels, nurturing her love for animals and solitude.

She has no plans of settling down anytime soon…

SassyZenGirl.com

Pinterest.com/SassyZenGirl
Instagram.com/SassyZenGirltravels
Facebook.com/SassyZenGirl
Youtube.com/c/SassyZenGirl
Twitter.com/SassyZenGirl

LuxuryPetCompanion.com

GundiGabrielle.com

55364274R00060

Made in the USA
Middletown, DE
09 December 2017